BAKER STREET LADIES

LEXI WOLFE

BAKER STREET
LADIES

First Printing, 2024
ISBN: 978-1-0685065-0-5
ISBN-13: 978-1-0685065-1-2

This play is dedicated to Artie Wolfe, my beloved,
long-suffering, wonderful husband, for whom this was the
first play of mine he ever saw.

I live in hope that I will someday find the words to tell you
how much you mean to me, and to adequately thank you
for all you are and do.

CONTENTS

AUTHOR'S NOTE

Dear Reader,

If you are reading, or possibly listening to this, you, like myself, are rather likely to be an avid Sherlock Holmes fan. If you're not, I'm flattered that you're reading this at all! Every care I can muster has gone into making sure that this play is both entertaining as a Sherlock homage and, forgiving artistic licence, is as true to the original canon as I can make it. However, I ask for your sympathy: I am but yet another indie writer and performer who is sharing one of my hyper-fixations with the world and moreover, happen not to be as capable as I was at such things since I developed fibromyalgia a few years ago, together with the worst of the curses that came with it - brain fog.

The Sherlock Holmes stories mean as much to me as they likely do to you, but I am without the luxury of editors or experts to weigh in, so I hope that you will enjoy my work for what it is and be able to forgive any potential oversights. I have added some very mild modern touches in terms of attitude, which I hope, while sadly not being true to the times the stories were set in, reflect in the best way both our own enlightenment and the feelings of validation many of us might be glad to find in a Holmes story.

Furthermore, I ask for your forgiveness that despite this work containing only women, and being fem-created, it nevertheless drastically fails the Bechdel Test for obvious reasons.

I have included stage directions, and descriptions, in the written version of the book, but for immersion's sake, I have left them out of the audio version. There will be discrepancies between stageplay and audiobook, as there was an unavoidable time lapse between the thing being created, and being committed to paper.

I hope you enjoy my minor contribution to the Holmesian universe and thank you for giving me, Mr. Holmes' stalker, Mary Morstan, Mrs. Hudson and a certain Irena Adler, your time and attention.

SCENE 1: GABRIELLA SHURGARD

In the street outside 221b Baker Street.

__An older lady with slightly eccentric wear is trying, unsuccessfully, to be subtle about approaching the front of the stage. She eventually addresses the audience as if taking a single person into her confidence. Her tact is wanting, but there is no mistaking her good nature and enthusiasm.__

Oh! I do beg your pardon there, I should have been paying more attention to where I was going! No, no, no harm done.

...Forgive me, I don't mean to be presumptuous, but you see, I couldn't help but notice just now that you've been meandering here in the street for a number of minutes and I rather wondered if you might be looking towards the upper windows on the other side of the street? The windows of one particular house, unless I am very much mistaken... No, no, my dear, no excuses need be made, no stories between friends, I assure you, for I have very much been in the exact same position in which you now find yourself. I understand all too well where in the journey you happen to be.

The specific windows that you seek, well... I can tell you exactly which they are without your needing to make it too obvious. I fancy no one has realised but I myself what you were about, but...

__She drops her voice.__

The very middle house on the opposite side of the street. Black railings and a black door. Not the square one, the one to the left of that with the transom window above it. The first floor above that, deep red curtains. I believe those are the windows that you might be looking for.

How do I know? Oh my dear, it's simplicity itself! Everyone who comes along Baker Street and has cause to stop about here does so for those windows. Unless, of course, they are looking for the door, but you seem not to have made up your mind yet?

Again, I do beg your pardon if I seem forward in my assumptions. I simply observed you for a moment or two, and said to myself "Aha! Here is someone whose purpose, in this street and at this very time, is one that I might discern without too much inquiry." Do correct me if I'm wrong, but are you not here to see... someone of note?

No, no, no - on second thoughts, don't answer - don't tell me a thing! I've been practising and you will do me a kindness by allowing me to use 'the usual methods' and tell me how close I came to the truth after!

Hmmm. Hmmm. Hmmm! Yes... Yes, a certain inquisitive look about the face. Semi-formal attire... Not the most expensive of outfits in one's wardrobe, one dare hope! Sensible er... footwear, I suppose. And a definite purpose in one's movement, I noticed as you walked down the street. Mmm. Mmm! Yes, indeed - I did think as much! I thought as soon as I saw you... and at this end of Baker Street at this hour - well, what else could one such as yourself be here for? You don't strike me as much of a local, dare I suggest, and I don't recall your face and if one had encountered it before, it is definitely a face one would remember. No! No, my dear friend, there is no need for you to say a word, I have seen, observed, and understood.

There's no escaping The Look. Those who are bound for 221b Baker Street seem unable to help themselves. Most people, strangely, unless their business is of a most urgent nature, find themselves standing here for a little time, marvelling up at those windows, hoping to catch a glimpse, knowing very well who lies beyond. Or sits, I suppose, at this time, for supper...

But now, if you would be so good - you may speak to me with absolute confidence and freedom, no matter how weighty the matter! You see, if you are indeed here to see a particular inhabitant of this row on good terms and obtain his services, why then, I daresay we are very much friends and acquaintances already!

Oh - for goodness sake! My excitement does make me forget my manners at times, I hope you'll pardon me. I wondered initially of course if I'd only be needed to supply directions - it's oddly easy to get disorientated on Baker Street on a busy evening such as this but - Mrs. Gabriella Ho - Shurgard. Gabriella Shurgard. Odd that we attach such significance to names even now. I have rooms just down the street, where I have my business, as it happens. Oh, and please don't fret if your visit and business necessitates great care and delicacy - I am the soul of discretion.

May I postulate? A sudden and inexplicable disappearance? A mysterious, unfathomable robbery, perhaps? A family matter, but involves some great mystery? Or perhaps an incomprehensible... murder? Do you suspect so much, but cannot prove it? Is there no motive, or no logical method? I can quite understand any hesitation, sharing any of it with someone who is all but a stranger, I really can, but, well, I'm sure you know it already, but if your conundrum is as good as solved in anyone's hands, it's -

Gracious! You do have an appointment, don't you? Oh, I'm afraid it's quite impossible to see Mr. Holmes if you haven't already made an appointment! I think it a great oversight that, no doubt for dramatic effect, the way Dr. Watson writes some of his tales - and I am not belittling his writing or his truthfulness whatsoever - one gets the impression that it must be quite easy to simply knock upon the door you see there, and more often than not, you will be ushered through the door and up the stairs at once! Ha! The sad reality is quite different. Mr. Holmes is these days very much in demand, you understand, and it is now near impossible to actually meet him straight away and he cannot be at home to everyone...

Oh, but now, don't despair. It is possible I may be able to do something for you. I am known at 221b. Should I see him my-self first, I promise to put in a word for you. At the earliest, I have an audience with him tomorrow, but I don't know if you can wait until then.

I'm not - recognisably - affiliated with Mr. Holmes. Not yet, no, but... Now you really must keep what I'm about to tell you to yourself, but, well, Mr. Holmes... and I...

She indicates in a way she might believe is subtle, and leaves a heavily pregnant pause for a moment, an atrocious knowing look and a conspiratorial grin on her face.

You shan't breathe a word? I can rely on you?

Oh do tell me, if you have time - I do so love hearing how others first came to know of him! Was it the publications? For myself as well - initially, anyway. I really rather wonder who I was, or perhaps who I thought I was, before Mr. Holmes. I can see myself now, and I would rather not. A carefree but unin-spired woman of society. A somewhat... uneventful life, rather commonplace, but I never knew it at the time. I suppose it was pleasant enough, one mustn't be ungrateful after all, but I had no more to do for the world than collect butterflies and attend very dull social events, with other very dull people, if you want my honest opinion! What I thought was happiness in my security was actually merely... ignorant contentedness. There was no real joy, no deep bliss... and really, what is life without genuine joy and happiness? Well, you'll believe in fate when I tell you this:

I'd never read Beeton in all my life. No! Not a single edition, not one. And yet, what do you suppose I was given on Christmas morning several years ago? Beeton's Christmas Annual. I read the story of 'A Study In Scarlet' in that same afternoon and as I did... I knew, somehow, even then, my life had been irrevocably altered. Perhaps I didn't know it as much as I felt it. I talked of nothing else over Christmas Dinner. As soon as Dr. Watson started writing the stories of Mr. Holmes in earnest, I ensured I was always the first to read them on our street, if not in the whole neighbourhood. And from that day to this, you shall find no one who knows the comings and goings of Mr. Holmes better than he himself and I. With the exception of Dr. Watson of course. Ah, happy times, when discoveries are freshly found.

Oh dear, I must be boring you... Well, after a little time, it became all too much for me, and I knew that I had to do something. Something radical, that I had never done before, to solidify my new sense of person, I felt it coming for weeks! Then, I read the name of a place that Mr. Holmes occasionally frequents and I couldn't help myself but to start patronising the place myself. When that sadly proved fruitless, I started having the carriage turn down this very street, even if my journey was in quite another direction. I once even was so bold, even in those early days, as to pass by the very door, two feet away from me at most. I knew then, just as I had somehow strangely known from the beginning, that Sherlock Holmes and I were destined to meet and to change one another's lives forever. And in this, in due course, I was right to have faith!

Trying to orchestrate a coincidental meeting, however, could be frightfully frustrating, and so I decided to... hurry Fate along. Now I didn't want to be like some of those appalling ridiculous creatures that try and secure his services for lost pencils and daughters who have probably simply run away to Gretna Green. I wasn't going to make up a case simply to get his attention. That is not how I do things. But I realised that, in much of his work, he has occasion to come into contact with other detectives. Why I didn't think of it before, I'll never know, but of course, the best way to meet a man who is so very devoted to his work, is surely to become as involved with the same line of work.

What do you think of the way I've styled myself? This is not what I'd call my natural look, you see, but I'm er... practising my in-cog-nito. *You'd be surprised what one can obtain when one is determined:* I thought it best to practice and what better subject to use as a starting point than the great man himself? The things I've found out and overheard. The things that in opportune moments - I can trust your discretion, can't I? Well, it's memorabilia. Some things that were probably thrown out in error but I can't bring myself to return, they've become precious to me. Even a thing or two that I ought ... Not to have...

Gabriella gives us the impression with this comment, with a look, that these objects might be somewhat... risque... Then carries on at once.

Oh listen to me, talking your ear off - I digress - I hit upon the idea of opening a consulting detective agency. My specialist line is to offer help to ladies who have dire and severe problems and cases in need of solving, but need the discretion of a fellow lady. My very first letter to Mr. Holmes was to inform him of this, and to ask if he had any advice to give, as well as if he would formally recognise us. It needn't be much, just asking Dr. Watson to put the name of the company in a story, or even to be quoted as saying that we were an agency to be watched out for. Nothing much. He does get an awful lot of post however. One morning, I saw him delivered of thirteen different letters. Thirteen, in one day! It's no wonder mine was lost in the shuffle.

If you should happen to go in before me, however, you should not pay too much attention to that landlady of his. Scottish, you know. Ghastly woman! Oh, I suppose that is too cruel - she must be a good sort, really - but she and I... have had a number of minor disagreements. Poor dear, she doesn't like change, one can tell, and ever since I've been here, she's been resisting it at every turn.

Oh! I haven't told you what you doubtless want to know the most, the best of it all - how I first met Mr. Holmes! Well, it was many months ago now. I'm acquainted with a lady who lives at Park Square, just around the corner from here - between you and I, she's not my favourite tea companion, talks a little too much - but I accepted an invitation to take tea and later made excuse that I had another call to make. A poorly cousin, that kind of thing. It was a pleasant day and something in my bones told me to walk instead of taking a carriage, so I had a leisurely stroll here. More fate, of course, because had I not, I might never have had the nerve to actually stop - just there! And before I knew another thing, a carriage pulled up behind me, I happened to turn and... there he was. Larger than life. Much larger, he's very tall. I tried to say something, but instead, I dropped my purse. Shock, I suppose. And he leant over and he picked it up, placing it back into my hands with such gentleness. "Your purse, madam," he said. And we stood like that for some little time and then he said: "Excuse me." He must have been as flustered as I, for he darted into the house before I could gather my wits even to thank him for his kindness.

That was only the first of many such little meetings, each one more meaningful than the next. Though, because of how important his work is, they have been few and fleeting. Do you know I very nearly knocked on the door again the other day? The man was looking at me down from the window - I saw him! Bold as you please! He looked directly at me, then of course pretended he looked elsewhere, and promptly vanished behind the curtain, but I saw his hand holding it for a moment, and that was when I knew for certain - it was a signal!

The first time it happened, I knocked on the door. I knew the landlady of course, by name, and I asked if Mr. Holmes was at home. The cheek she employed when she told me, quite plainly, that she was unsure and would I like to leave my card, but it may take some time for Mr. Holmes to reply. I told her, she knew very well that Mr. Holmes was upstairs and no, I would not leave a card - I was to be taken to see him immediately. She gave me a very withering look and asked me to wait. She eventually reappeared and had the audacity to tell me that Mr. Holmes was in the middle of some very important and delicate business, and sent his apologies. I tried to keep composure, knowing that though I could not yet understand it, this was all a wonderful, great, detailed plan of his: it's the only explanation. I said graciously that I was willing to accept this delay in our meeting, and that she should pass onto him *The Letter*. The one I told you of, the consulting agency. I had written it out again, realising that the first letter must have been lost. She was rather bemused. She asked if it were the particulars of the case I wished to put before him. I lost my head with the giddiness of the moment: "I am the person Mr. Holmes is seeking.". And then I left. The woman's face was such a picture!

She threatened me with the police the other week. Can you imagine? She came out with some great tale - that she had been specifically instructed not to let 'my type' into the house. I ask you! Perhaps she has her own designs on him after all; you know she's a widow. I wouldn't put it past the realms of possibility. After all - do you know this one by heart as I do? - 'When you have eliminated both the possible and the impossible, whatever remains, however improbable, must be the truth.' He's really quite a character, my Sherlock, even when you know him very well.

My husband had his concerns. In the beginning, he was all encouragement, of course: 'Those stories are a godsend, she leaves me alone now when I am at home, none of this infernal witter'. Ah, Victor, so little did you realise. But soon, it was 'My god, woman, can't you make conversation about anything else but that dratted Holmes character?' Not long after that, he started the slander. I suppose spurned men are wont to do such things. He said I was obsessed, that there was something terribly wrong with me - how very convenient - but in the end, it was just too cruel. I had to tell him. That Mr. Holmes and I had met, that I had been called upon to have a career of my own, and that our marriage was over. He didn't take it well. There was shouting first, and then there were silences and disbelieving expressions, but noticeably, no tears. I told him That as much as proved I was now doing the right thing, and I asked that he support me in whatever way he felt he could during what was to be a naturally difficult time. I found the rooms down the road from here and took them without even looking at them. Even as I was taking all the things one holds most precious to the carriage, in order that I might begin anew, he was talking still, pleading that I 'see sense', as if any of it could make a difference. I eventually answered him: 'Victor, my dear, I believe that for the first time, I am seeing things in greater clarity than I have ever seen them before.' I do feel pity - any sane man might find it difficult, to understand, suddenly, after nearly thirty years together, our marriage is over. "For god's sake," he kept saying, "what on earth am I to tell the children?"

He has written letters since. Refuses to grant me a divorce until I have been properly 'assessed by a medical professional'. He's going to plead that I must be insane for leaving him, I suppose. I told my children to write, but as yet they're refusing. I had at least thought the elder ones would write to express their understanding, but they seem to all have something against me and my happiness. I always did completely right by them. Looking after Victor and his household, bringing up all five of his children, sacrificing years of my life for my family's well-being - but it is very telling, is it not? The moment I find true happiness, I am no more than a traitor in their midst.

Forgive me, I don't wish to speak of What Was any more. For me now, there is only all that is to come.

It is tiring, however. Grievous, in fact, to be the woman whom cannot be named, who cannot be publicly acknowledged. I know truly that it will all be worth it in the end, but I do grow impatient. No, indeed, I have kept my distance. It is the sensible thing to do. The right thing to do. I even practiced on Dr. Watson a few days ago. I bumped into him, or rather I had been walking a certain pace behind him for a good few hundred yards, when I was suddenly overtaken with boldness and thought I ought to introduce myself to him. He will know me well enough hereafter.

"Can I help you, Madam?" says he.

"I'm grateful to you sir," I answered, "but no, I don't believe so. I fear it is your acquaintance Mr. Holmes who I am seeking."

"Ah, yes?" said he with innocence and cheer. "You could tell me a little something of the matter, if you wanted it said to him."

"No, no," I protested firmly, "again, so kind of you, but I fear only the ears of the man himself will hear what I have to say."

"Forgive me, Madam, but did you happen to come to 221b some time ago and speak to Mrs. Hudson, asking to be brought straight up?"

"I did indeed." Now, I think, now he must know who I am.

"Mrs. Shurgard."

"Not for very much longer," I corrected him. "But I see you've been told of me."

"I have," he said. "Your husband was most insistent I see you."

I was taken aback by this obvious subterfuge. "I do not tolerate trickery, sir, and I fear my husband is employing nothing but just now, in order to thwart any semblance of happiness I attempt to afford myself."

"You misunderstand," he told me. "Your husband has told me much about you. If I am able, indeed, I want to help."

"You can help me, sir, by escorting me to 221b Baker Street and delivering me to your friend whom we both know all too well immediately. The housekeeper lady is behaving like little more than a guard dog with the crown jewels with me!"

There was some different talk back and forth and then he said: "I'll tell you what I can do for you. I do have a friend who... specialises in cases such as yours. If I were to make an appointment for the two of you to meet, at my practice..."

Oh my dear, the sudden realisation - I had been a fool! All the time, Dr. Watson had obviously been my friend and was continuing Mr. Holmes' need for secrecy, for enabling us to meet fully, in private, at last! I understood at once what lay beneath his coded words - a friend who specialises in 'cases such as mine'. So suddenly, there it was. A card in my hand, his own name, a pseudonym that was obviously being employed for his 'friend', tomorrow's date and a time. And it was arranged. Just like that. I'm to see Dr Watson and his 'friend' first thing in the morning. .. Do you think it tasteless if a woman wears white when she is married a second time? I was thinking more ivory, possibly even cream instead...

Oh my dear, I am so very sorry; how long I have kept you! You must be eager to get in and I've thoughtlessly babbled through your composure time! Now, let me tell you this - he may use his signals with you, thinking you are me, and you will not know: if the curtain does not twitch at all, he cannot see you. If it twitches just once, it might be doable, if twice, he is trying his best to arrange it and if the window opens fully... No, has that ever been...? No, my imagination. Anyway, my dear - of course, of course - so good to meet you, I have enjoyed speaking with you, and if you do get in, do me the greatest of services and tell him - no - say... that there is someone greatly looking forward to our appointment - I mean - the appointment with Dr. Watson's friend, 'Freud' tomorrow. You'll do that, won't you, dear? Well, I'll leave you be. My very best wishes to you and I hope you can say the same to me on my happy day. Don't worry, you're invited - half of London will want to be there, I've no doubt.

Oh! Did you see that! There is someone up there - go, go quickly! I'll see you soon, no doubt!

SCENE 2 : MISS MARY MORSTAN / MRS JOHN WATSON

In the hall of 221b.

As the lights come up on the elegant but sparse Victorian entrance hall, complete with an accent chair to one side, there is the sound of footsteps approaching as if descending the stairs.

A lady in her mid-to-late 20s appears, somewhat out of breath and clearly in minor distress. At first, she does not notice the audience until she takes a few steps forward as if to leave, then -

Oh. Good evening. I beg your pardon, I was just about to leave. Are you here to...

I don't know why I ask, of course you're here to see Mr. Holmes, hardly anyone comes through the door that isn't. I'm afraid he's not at home just now. I only just arrived myself, really...

I'm terribly sorry - Do we know each other? I don't suppose you were brought up in India? Schooled in Edinburgh? No?

Oh, no, of course, it was the - exactly! We met there. How could I have forgotten? That must be a number of years ago, however: I trust you've been well since then? I'm no longer Miss Mary

Morstan, these days I'm rather Mrs. John Watson. I came to see if my husband was to be found here, but it seems he's not...

Her eyes seem to roll momentarily and she reaches out to steady herself, falling into the chair onstage. She uses the chair continually, between rising at points and sitting when she feels overcome or emotional.

Oh dear. Forgive me, I! Oh dear, I thought I should have to sit down. No, no, no, please don't be alarmed, I'm quite alright. A little too much exertion today though. I'm - I'm sorry, do sit down. Mrs. Hudson will likely be through with some tea before too long. She's very good like that. Oh dear me. Well I suppose one uninterrupted and planned dinner date at home was a little too much to ask. Forgive me, I'm talking to myself, I suppose. You see, it's erm...

It's our anniversary today. I arranged a little something. I did ask John if it was going to be too much. If there was anything that he knew Mr. Holmes might be working on and likely to ask for his help, during. If he'd said Yes, I would have understood and simply arranged another evening. I didn't like to draw his attention to the date; he has so many other things on his mind. "But really," I said, "if you think it would be possible..."

"Nothing would delight me more," he said. "I know that I can't always, for a number of reasons, but... This time, I shall make the time."

A sad pause of reflection on this broken promise.

I've known Mr. Holmes as long as I've known my husband. I could not have said that I was under illusions. I knew - one could tell - from the beginning that their friendship was an incredibly important connection. I suppose I underestimated just how important it was to each of them.

Do you know, they sometimes remind me of something my father once said when I was quite a child: He was an army man, a Captain. I had noticed how attached he was to the soldiers he served with. Almost like they were brothers. I asked him, strangely, if he'd loved my mother so much, and here he took me on his knee and said: "Mary, there are some things you may understand and some you might never. Some people marry their soulmate. Some don't. Some can't. Some people don't have one. But some have friends, wherein they find the same feeling.." Words to that effect.

I believe my John has that with Mr. Holmes. I think Mr. Holmes has that with John, whether he knows it or not. I wish I knew what that was like.

I'm beginning to feel a little better already. I do hope I didn't startle you. I've been under the weather recently, and I was so hoping they'd be here. But if they are out together, they could be, quite genuinely, anywhere on God's green earth.

Awkward, brief pause.

I have an aunt I see sometimes. Second cousin relation. The last time I visited, it was supposed to be the two of us, but at the last minute, the plan changed. 'Mary, I don't know how you tolerate it. If I were you, I'd...' She didn't actually tell me what she'd do, but I suppose it's because she wouldn't know what to do. Somewhat like myself. I don't know what to do.

I have never, not for an instant - (**brief pause - this is a lie**) - resented Mr. Holmes and his sway over my husband and his ever-moving calendar. It was he that enabled us to meet, after all. I could tell, of course, that there was an attraction, when John and I met. I have always told him I don't know what it was, but I do. Many daughters of Army Men marry Army Men, but I didn't want to. I thought, somehow, by marrying a doctor who had once been an Army Man instead, I wouldn't be so worried about where he was all the time and how long he'd be away, and would know that he would be back safely with me before the day was done.

Love does make us all short-sighted, so I am informed. I had such wonderful ideas. John was going to run his practice and after we wed, Mr. Holmes would soon be able to find someone who was not so... tied to others to rely upon. We'd read of him in the papers, and occasionally, he might even come to supper, and regale John with all that was happening in his absence. John would scribble down notes at the table, and promise to write it up, and I would smile while I heard many stories across the dinner table, and never complain, even if I'd heard them more than once before. They would argue, as they do now, how such a thing happened and how it was known... Mr. Holmes would admit, subtly, that he wished John would join him on some of his escapades once more. John would smile fondly and take my hand and say with quiet assurance, 'Thank you, my dear Holmes, but I fear I have other responsibilities now.' After a few years, children. Boys, definitely. One to name Arthur after my father and I can think of worse names than Sherlock. I'm sure John would approve. So he with his patients, and me finding patience to bring up some children, we would continue our lives in a quiet, dignified way, watch our children grow and... grow old together. We'd sit reading in the evening. I'd read his own stories back to him in the twilight of our lives when our children had left home. Here and there say "What a clever turn of phrase, my dear," and occasionally ask, do you miss it? And he'd grin and say: Yes. And No.

It's strange. Sometimes, especially when you fall in love, you see more of the person that you believe them to be, rather than the person they truly are, who may be hiding behind your love.

We had a quiet honeymoon. I believe it was several days after our return that John dashed off a note from the practice. 'I'm sorry, my dear - Holmes has need of me. I shall let you know that I am alright, but don't expect me for supper. If it's going to be a few days, I'll endeavor to let you know.' I remember holding the note and thinking 'Oh, how sweet of him, that he lets me know. That he apologises.'

I still didn't see it. He was gone for a few days. I took charge of a small child while her parents had business. Pleasant girl. I was a governess before my marriage but now, I started to wonder what it would be to have my own. By the time the child left and John returned, I knew I wished it, more than anything. Mr. Holmes could have John here and there for now, but my next big adventure was going to be motherhood.

Weeks and even a month or two might go by and the only thing I knew of Mr. Holmes was what I read in John's stories. Then out of the blue, he'd disappear! A note or a message would arrive. Sometimes, he'd even come home to fetch his revolver. I've always hated that gun because it meant he was going into danger. I became rather good at holding my tongue. I wanted to say 'John, for god's sake: is it worth the risk? Please, put that down, and stay at home.' But I didn't. And it wouldn't stop me worrying.

It was easy to think that as soon as things 'settled down', somehow, all would be right. This time last year, I was making arrangements again for our anniversary. And I came down in the morning and there was the note waiting for me in the hall. I got

a feeling as I looked at it like it was a bad luck omen, that kept re-
curring and coming back to me each time I gave it away. I didn't
even read it, I knew it was an apology, a brief explanation of very
little and possibly a vague idea of where he might be.

That was the moment I realised. He hadn't even realised the
date. My dreams, which had seemed so crystal clear of what was
to come, were nothing more than dreams, even though they were
so simple. If there was to be an arrangement in which one of the
three of us was going to be a third person to a party, it was not
Mr. Holmes in our marriage... I wonder it took me so long to understand and I wish I'd known who said it: 'You can't change a
man you marry. You can try, and both of you can be miserable,
or you can leave himself to himself and find your happiness in
other things.'

The whole day, I stayed in bed, as if someone had died, which
it almost felt as if they had. On his return, I pulled myself together very sharply... Why on earth did I think that I'd have an
effect of change? Why did I think I'd make the difference? I just
assumed. I didn't even realise what it meant, I just assumed.

Please don't misunderstand - we have been very happy together. We are very happy together. I suppose a husband ex-
pects a wife to look after herself, and to look after her own
feelings too.

Still, I prayed for a child. I would be present and fight for my
health, to be there for my own children as my mother never could
be. Yet the more I thought of it, I felt that when the child was
born, things would change between John and I. I only really con-
sidered a few days ago, when... when I perceived changes in myself.

I suddenly wondered what on earth I should say to my child when John would disappear for days on end. And to my horror, I heard my own voice. Asking as a child for my father. Not knowing that I would never see him again. Suddenly, I felt this awful feeling of impending danger. Not just for John crawling through bushes and taking his revolver everywhere. For our children. What would I have said to them?

So I wrote him a note. I reminded him of the importance of the date and that, if at no other point in the immediate future, he must be here for this. I was going to tell him. Tell him our news. Then I was going to find the strength from somewhere deep within me, locked away like a precious stone in a safe, and tell him that as soon as he was a father, things would have to change. I could not have a child of mine being brought up in ignorance about their father. I can see myself with tears in my eyes, pleading with him, telling him what it is to have a parent so very far away, so that one barely knows oneself. That has plagued me my entire life...

And I can't imagine what he might've answered. Now I shall never know. I left the note in his inside coat pocket, just sticking out enough that he would find it. "I believe," I wrote at the end, "I shall have something very important to tell you this evening and then we must have a discussion of what the future holds."

I found the note on the floor in the hall. It must have fallen from his pocket when he dashed out to wherever; it was unopened. I'm very glad of that now.

I was in the consulting room this afternoon, in fact. I struggled not to grin as I informed the doctor of my name and why I had come. He asked why I'd not spoken to my own husband. It sort of caught me off-guard.

"My husband is busy," I answered.

And he nodded. It almost felt he should say something more, but he didn't. It never struck me before that my husband's reputation always preceded him. This doctor didn't ask what he was doing, where he was - anything of that nature. He just nodded. He knew, as much as I did where he was and who with. And I suddenly felt this afternoon, for the first time, really, properly, truly - shut out.

I didn't tell him. I didn't tell him that I hadn't wanted to tell John, nor for John to find it out on his own. I had wanted to announce it and for just a few moments, if nothing more when he found it out, he, I, our marriage and what was to come from it were to be the most important things in his world. A few moments was all I felt it right to demand, but I wanted them...

The doctor listened quietly for a moment, then asked me some questions. Asked about my eating habits. How much I slept and if I were normally quite as fatigued as I appeared. Where I ached the most and if my weight had changed. A line started to grow between his brows. And that was the first moment I was conscious that it was also possible I was wrong. "It's not good news, is it?" I asked. He met me with silence.

Just tonight, John. Just tonight.

The doctor asked when I could tell John. I said I didn't know, but I was expecting to see him tonight. "It ought to be discussed fairly soon," he told me. What a gentle manner. Exactly that which I fell for John for.

He usually sends a note if he is going to be gone for very long. I've no doubt that if I were to tell him, he'd come back, but... But he has been so very good to me. After my father, he's quite been one of the best things to happen to me in my life. He shall be the love of my life.

And so, I must therefore try to forgive him for the fact that I am not his.

This last great personal confrontation made, Mary rises from the seat for the last time, fiddling to put gloves on as she prepares to hold her head high as she leaves.

I do wonder what's kept Mrs. Hudson. No, no, don't get up, please, I've kept you and my carriage waiting long enough, I'm so sorry. I'm glad you were here this evening. It's been very good to see a friendly face and talk. If, by any remote chance, they do return while you're still here, you shan't say anything? Thank you.

Well, I have my own house to be getting to. I hope whatever it is you're here for, you get it seen to very soon. How nice to see you again. Do take care of yourself. And... thank you.

SCENE 3 : MRS. HUDSON

In Sherlock's rooms at 221b.

The stage is in mild disarray. It has all the trappings of an elegant Victorian drawing room (complete with an extra Persian slipper hanging by the fireplace and the bulletholes 'V R' in the wall) but with teacups, sheet music, newspaper, forgotten trays of supper and other paraphernalia littering the floors and surfaces. A large armchair sits like a proud island amidst the chaos.

Mrs. Hudson, a robust Scottish lady bustles into the room, looking harangued and on a mission. It takes her a moment to realise she's not alone.

Oh! Oh, you didn't half give me fright, I didn't think there was anyone up here! Did you have an appointment? You may be waiting a while, just to let you know.

Oh my goodness, another ruined dinner(!) I no longer suffer surprise, after all this time. "Will you be in for dinner, Mr. Holmes?" "I'm afraid I couldn't say, Mrs. Hudson." "Well, what kind of thing shall I put on the stove just in case you are home, Mr. Never-At-Holmes?" "Anything you like, Mrs. Hudson, anything you like."

It's enough to turn your hair grey. I don't know how he survived before he had someone to do for him, but then I suppose he did as all men do - they had women! His mother, and no doubt an army of maids to clean up and clear out and cook and mend and put right and pull bullets out of walls and pick needles, ash and God alone knows what else up off the floor.

My goodness. What a life! I tell you something, I never foresaw any of this when I had two young gentlemen turn up at my door asking to look at the rooms all those years ago. Oh dear, if only I could talk to my younger self. I'd say, "Martha, dear, you're a fool for taking them at face value." Well, I could tell they weren't rogues and they could afford the rates. Mr. Holmes whipped through here like he was trying to get away from a wasp, inspecting everything. I suppose he can't help himself. He seemed pleasant enough if a little blunt, but then you expect that from the upper classes. It's the ones that aren't pleasant either, that make me hope that someday, we too may get the vote!

Anyway, 'Oh yes, this will do quite nicely,' he tripped out here and there, and then he goes into one bedroom and I hear him mutter. 'Oh. Oh no no no, this will never do.' At which point Dr. Watson says 'Don't worry, Holmes, that can be my bedroom, see if you like the other better.' And he did. But it was Dr Watson trying to hide his limp that really did for me. A surgeon who'd done his duty and has paid a permanent price in mobility, in Afghanistan, and who wanted nothing more than to settle back down and have a nice comfortable life, running a practice for the benefit of others, while living with a friend.

At least, I always assumed they were friends. You, er... you hear some things in London, some arrangements made you'd never even know existed if you'd ended up living somewhere between Stirling and Paisley like everyone thought I might. Though I knew a thing or two. I've a cousin, Geraldine, she came to visit me and brought her boy Fabian with her a while back. Fabian was very eager to visit London, and went off to amuse himself, but his mother was beside herself.

"Martha," she says, "I cannae do a thing with him. He doesn't want to get married. Have you ever heard such a thing? Girls, he knows plenty, but he is only ever friends with them. There's something unnatural, though, when he meets a pleasant-looking young man, and I'm at the end of my tether knowing what to do about it."

Now maybe by this time I'd been too long in London, think as you will, but I said to her: "When you say unnatural, Geraldine, what is it that's gone wrong?"

"I'm sure I don't know," she wails.

"Well, what of his brother, is he unnatural?"

"Oh, no, he got married last spring."

"Well then. And did you do anything that might have made your boy unnatural, do you suppose?"

"Oh no, nothing of the kind, me nor his father, we both dote upon the boy!"

"Well, that's good enough! And what of Fabian? Do you suppose he's done something himself, to make him the way he is?"

"Oh no, in all other respects, he's such a good boy."

"Well then," says I, "it doesn't sound like it can be unnatural after all! And may I quote to you, Geraldine, that the Lord works in mysterious ways and we are not to know his purpose, or all the things that he created and why, and from everything you've said to me, Geraldine, I don't think our Fabian is unnatural after all." Oh dear, I am wittering, it does happen increasingly, these days.

Anyway, it was in 1881 that they came. Oh dear, if only I could talk to my younger self. I'd say, "Martha, these men look like ten-ants. But one is a disguised nightmare."

There were things I could overlook in the beginning. People coming and going, more than I was used to - I had to replace my hall carpet - and some very strange habits. Now I'm not the world's best cook, I don't pretend to be, I don't believe in all these unnecessary pieces of leaves all over your supper, but sometimes Mr. Holmes would eat well and hearty and other times, you'd think I was trying to poison him. Whole days he'd go without touching a morsel, no wonder he's so thin, but I'd know all was well if I heard him playing the fiddle. I love a good fiddle. But not at half past four in the morning. I went up to his door still with my nightcap on, knocked and found the Doctor already up, wav-ing some kind of needle about and down talking Mr. Holmes very sternly, so I left them to it, but he did not leave off playing for over an hour. And that was only the beginning.

One day, I'd just put my hands in the sink when a crash, loud enough to wake my dearly departed husband from his slumber blew through the house. I shrieked and dropped one of my best plates. I heard several noises exactly the same after that, then some silence, then more. I thought something awful was happen-ing, and when I finally pluck up the courage to ascend the stairs, Mr. Holmes is there in his rooms with a gun pointing at my wall-paper that hadn't been up two years.

As if that wasn't bad enough, you couldn't see the floor for how many papers, books, clothes and even cups of tea that littered it. I said 'This is the very last straw, Mr. Holmes," and he had the nerve to bring me into the room and show me that the bullets spelled out 'VR' for Victoria Regina.

"Mr. Holmes there are a great many ways of being patriotic, but shooting at my bricks and mortar does not seem a very sensible one. Out he came with something clever to shut me up, but the problem was the next time he paid his rent, it was triple. 'For the inconvenience', he said to me. Now that's my problem, if someone's paying you honestly, and even more than you should rightly be taking, you shouldn't look a gift horse in the mouth. I thought at the time, I'll never be able to get another tenant in after this. Huh! If only I could talk to my younger self! I'd say: "Martha, solely because this strange gentleman has taken up living in your home previously, they'd snap your hand off for the address. And besides, he doesn't look like he'll ever leave."

Oh dear me. They never think of me either. Oh they'll pass the time of day and ask me how I am and I've never faulted either of them for how gentlemanly they are, but the things you hear. The people who barge their way into my home because they've an issue with Mr. Holmes. I've shown people into this house that have murdered their spouses, their relatives, and they look just like everybody else. The money wasted on food untouched, but apparently it's because I have a limited cuisine. But the worst is not knowing, or worse still, half knowing.

Apart from all my cousins, all of whom have stayed north of the border like anyone sensible would, I suppose I don't really have anyone. It was always Mr. Hudson and me and it suited us. And then, God rest his soul, when he passed, I knew not where to turn. I thought of going home, but to what? To relatives, to be a burden on them in time to come? No, no. I used the money that

I got after he died to buy the rest of the house so that I could have an income and feel useful.

My cousin Brian - I'm always losing track of how many cousins I really have - he came to visit me just before and about a few years after Mr. Sherlock Holmes came to live here. At first he said: "Martha, what are you about? You'll have the worst sort of villains, or people really down on their luck to rent here, why not sell the whole thing and come home?" But I didn't want to. He changed his tune the next time. You see Brian is a member of the local constabulary in our part of the world and naturally, he had come to hear of Mr. Holmes. They met very briefly and Brian, over our dinner that night says to me:

"You can tell, he's got that thing."

"What thing?" I asked.

"You know. The Thing... Like Emmet had. He may be alright in himself but he's...-...different."

"I don't think you'll find anyone more different than Mr. Sherlock Holmes," I said.

"Ay, that's what I mean. The things that make him different are actually the same things that make him brilliant. Now, there's some as'll say that it's so different, it's got no place, but here's the thing. Mr. Holmes being the way he is, and doing what he does that members of my constabulary, much higher up than I, have a good opinion of him and are seeking his advice, well, I say there is a place in this world for it. No. I go beyond it. I say such differences are necessary, in a world such as ours."

We've had more than our share of differences, Mr. Holmes and myself. I find him at times incredibly trying, and very reckless. He puts himself in danger, and the Doctor, and I don't think it's right, but I can't fault his results, because when he goes after something, he gets it. But they do never think of me. I'm just the mithering old woman back at Baker Street who worries herself witless some nights, thinking over and over of all the terrible things that could befall 'em. I understand that they don't rightly think, but who else should I worry for? God rest his soul, Mr. Hudson is no longer with us. My cousins, however many there are of them, I almost never see. But I have two gentlemen, one of whom still lives upstairs and another who is here now perhaps more often than when he lived here with us. I suppose I look on Mr. Holmes as a kind of son. And I do worry. Maybe it's selfish, or dread, I don't know. Dread because I don't want to awake one morning to find that the one person to whom I've given a little part of my life to is no longer there. And selfish, I suppose because you do have all kinds coming and going, and he entertains everyone who he finds interesting or suspicious, and what should I do if I come in to offer him tea one afternoon and find him... And no one in the world who'd know what'd happened, only he himself knowing how to solve such a thing. I couldn't bear it. Really, it's the dread of that kind of thing that keeps me awake at night.

You wouldn't know Mr. Holmes had any worries whatsoever, but he does. He's been very secretive recently. I have worried if someone's after him. That was also why I started when I came in and found you in here. I think he's up to something, but I don't know what. With Mr. Holmes, as with so many men like him, you never know his true mind. You can guess it, but you don't know if it's actually right or if it's what he wants you to think. I can't think what he might be up to. He's been sending a lot of letters. Mind you, he has for a number of years now. He never used to send so many. I thought at one point maybe he'd finally met someone. Whatever it is, it's going to be more convoluted than anything I could imagine, I know that.

No, something's bothering him. After ten years of living with that man over my head, that at least, I can tell. He still has a number of cases - it's when he doesn't you want to watch out - but I wonder how much he feels fulfilled by them. I've opened his post at his bidding before - 'Oh it's bound to be full of trivialities, please read it to me, Mrs. Hudson' and I have. He scoffs at some of the letters... I've kept one or two back. He may not appreciate that others think so highly of him now, but someday, he'll be glad of my keeping just some of them back instead of putting them on the fire. 'I am not interested in the letters of my fanatics', he'd likely say. But someday, Mr. Holmes, you and I both know that that may well be all you have.

It was not long after the Doctor left us to go and live with Mrs. Watson after they got married when I caught Mr. Holmes unaware. He didn't have a case, I don't think and I went in after not seeing him for a day or two, expecting him to be in one of his awful moods. Instead he's just sitting there with his violin, looking very melancholy. When he looked up and saw I was there, he tried to pull himself together, but I'd seen what I'd seen. We'd talked about things that we weren't talking about. I asked him if he was any better, in which I was asking if it was that he was missing the doctor. And he said 'passably', which I suppose was a yes. I asked him if he wanted any tea, which was my way of asking if there was anything else the matter that I may help with. And he said, no, but thank you. Which was as much as I could ever get out of him. Then, as I stand in the doorway to leave, I hear him say:

"Mrs. Hudson, what is your favourite piece of music?"

I tell you straight, I've never been asked before, Mr. Holmes.

"Well, I'm asking you now. What's your favourite piece of music?"

And I don't know, but even though I thought to say 'Don't be silly, man, just you put that violin away and let's have some quiet, I can always bring up a little something, and you can sleep on whatever it is that's troubling you', instead I said: "Well, Mr. Holmes, when I was a girl I used to go to a Dance, and at that very same dance, I met my late husband. There was one tune they played towards the end of the evening, and I always danced to it. It was called something like a Selling Round?"

'I know the tune you mean. It's a folk song.'

"Really? Well, I don't know anything else and so - that's my favourite piece, I suppose. Goodnight, Mr. Holmes."

And I went downstairs and I hadn't even gotten into my own room, when for just a wee while, I heard these notes floating down from above me, and I was taken back to when I was young and dancing with the boy who'd become my husband. If I'd not felt so silly, I'd have probably danced there on the landing. And I thought, as I went into the bedroom, that had I not been there at that dance that night, I might never have met him. He wouldn't have had the idea to move us to London and almost none of my life that has happened, would've, and that that would have been quite a shame, for what else would I have done?

Ah, if only I could talk to my younger self. I'd tell myself:

Martha. You'll reach a certain age when that lovely young man is no longer with you and you're on your own and make the decision to take in tenants. From that day, you'll be run ragged, shouted at, told you're underfoot and that ye cannae cook. You're upstairs will never be tidy, one tenant will not leave the house for weeks and then not come home for weeks, and you'll develop such a worry whether they are dead or alive, and it'll be nothing to do with the rent! You'll be sworn to secrecy, you'll be enlisted to help on cases for the empire itself, and then you'll still have to make doubly sure that there's enough ham and eggs for break- fast in the morning. There'll be strangers and all sorts coming in and out of that dearly purchased house of yours. If you're lucky, you'll hear the odd snatch of conversation, and only learn what it was all about through reading of it much later, and be very glad you didn't know it at the time. Kings and murderers, millionaires and street urchins will traipse through that door of yours, at all hours of the day and night, and if all that doesn't keep you awake, the fiddle certainly will.

But Martha dear, though nobody says it, maybe it is that no one even realises the little things you do, for it's easy to overlook the little things in times of turmoil, you will never feel more im- portant in all your life. We can't all be heroes, is what my father said to me. But helping heroes, well, that's about as important a work as you can otherwise do in the world. You won't feel it all the time, but there'll be moments when you even feel grateful that you were given the opportunity to do the very best you could when it mattered. And Martha, when you are able to do that, you will never in all your life feel more proud and alive.

Well my goodness gracious me, here I am with some cold tea in front of me. Why don't I go downstairs and brew a pot? If you don't mind waiting, I can always pop into the cellar, and see if I have a drop or two to make it all the sweeter, if you see what I mean. Give me a moment, I'll pop downstairs and see what we've got. Make yourself at home.

SCENE 4 : MRS. NORTON / IRENA ADLER

The lights dim minutely on Sherlock's sitting room.

Approaching footsteps, a door opens with a creak, and then an elegantly dressed woman enters furtively, looking fearful of being caught. She sneaks halfway across the stage before she suddenly realises she is not alone, and stops dead in her tracks. A pause. She mutters in frustration:

Damn.

She shows no fear of being caught - rather annoyance. She at once assumes authority over the space and is quick with a knowing smile.

Hmm. Good evening.

He's not at home then? No, I was afraid he wouldn't be. Have you been waiting long?... Forgive me for coming in by stealth, it was just that I wanted to avoid the housekeeper - is she the housekeeper? Or is she the landlady? You know, I've never been sure...

I don't suppose you mind if I wait with you for a little time? Though somehow I think both of us are going to be disappointed.

Thank you. So kind.

__She sits herself for the moment in the armchair, getting out a cigarette and matchbox. When she looks towards the audi-ence, she has a glimmer of superiority which is almost unset-tling about her. She never sits in the chair for very long.__

Cigarette? Never mind, strangers and all that, I understand. I presume you don't mind if I...?

You're one of his clients, then. Forgive me for stating the obvious, but I guess you must be desperate if you're waiting this late. Almost as desperate as that poor creature I saw outside. Did you see a large woman, older, on your way in? She's still there. She didn't see me, or I daresay I wouldn't have been able to get away. (*Beat of laughter*) Odd to think Sherlock - 'Mr. Holmes' now has a little of what I used to have.

Oh, of course - I'm terribly sorry, if there's one thing I should have learned from all my time in your country, it's that your countrymen are far more formal than mine - it's, er, Norton. Mrs. Irena Norton.

Odd. It's been several years now, and I still can't get used to that name. It would have a certain prestige over here, I guess. My husband was a very well-known and respected lawyer. Godfrey Norton, you may have heard of him. Emigrated a few years ago?

Back when I met him, my name was Adler.

Hmm. I see you've heard of me. I shan't ask if it was before or after the story.

Forgive me - How long have you been waiting, exactly? It just looks as if the answer might be 'a while'. So what are you here to see him for? Oh! Wait - of course - discretion.

Why am I here? Well as I sit here, I realise that before I got here, I knew, and now...

Well, I knew one of two things was going to happen when I came through that door. That either he would have done as he said and - he wouldn't be here or otherwise, the whole thing would be a ruse and he'd be here, lying in wait. Well, I had to know. And it's not like I'm going to let anyone else have all the fun any more.

You know, a few years ago, when I first left this cold and dreary island - no offence, of course - I assumed that was our business concluded. I mean, between myself and Mr. Sherlock Holmes. I'd never see him again. Despite his being, unbeknownst to me, best man and witness at my recent wedding, I was now, in a way, on the run from him. So Godfrey and I, armed with very little really, crossed the waters, disembarked, got to our new house... And the day after we arrived, what do you suppose was waiting on the doormat, but a letter. Addressed to me. You'll never guess who it was from.

He's a very resourceful man, really. I had a chance to stop it there, and I should've. I should have burnt it, unopened - I knew who it was from - but damn my curiosity. How did he know?

When I eventually opened it, the letter explained - a series of small but fascinating tricks that he knew I would be interested to hear, and then he asked that I reply to him. Just to settle a wager with himself that he'd be able to find me. He talked about keeping himself sharp, and if I didn't respond, then he'd know that he had misjudged or made an error in his deductions somewhere.

Hmm. Oh, I put it off for days, weeks... Replying. Godfrey was confident there was no cause to extradite us, and so he laughed at my preoccupation with the letter. 'Burn it and be done', he told me.

But I couldn't. Instead, I kept it in my desk, thinking about how Sherlock Holmes would be assuming that once again, I had somehow sidestepped his intelligence. I wanted him to think that he'd got it wrong. That he could make analyses without assumption and find the most intricate answers to things no one else could, but for all that, he couldn't understand me.

I was so angry when I realised I was lying to both of us.

However, I had no need of him. I put aside my personal rule that no man was done with me until I said so, and thought my husband must be right. To draw the thing, finally, to a close. So I wrote him a postcard. The picture was a view very like that, that I saw from my window each morning when the curtains were opened. I like to imagine his face when he got it.

Now, I decided, we were done. I could settle down in peace with my new life and my new husband, Sherlock Holmes could go back to doing whatever it is he does. I could be happy in my way, he in his...

Those first months, back home with Godfrey? They were wonderful. I didn't have to do anything I didn't want to do. For someone like me, born into my circumstances, you don't know what that's like. All women, I think, have to do things that they really don't want to do sometimes, but... suddenly, I had Godfrey. I was a happily married woman. I was looked after. Godfrey had a good profession and he was good at it, and I had all the time in the world to decide what to do with myself next...

You see, Godfrey didn't keep me or see me as other men view their wives. From the first moment he heard me speak, and heard something that spoke to him deeper than even I intended my words, he must've seen me as the grandest of prizes. That's why he fought so valiantly for me - dedicated, uprooted and rehomed his entire life for me. He loved me. I him. For the first time, for the last time like it. And in those giddy moments in the beginning, when husbands and wives are friends as well, we had talked and played games with one another. I've always loved games, but what Godfrey set up for me; how he said I could help his work, it was like nothing I'd ever had to entertain me before.

"My love. You are a criminal, but a person of great breeding and birth as well. You have recently fallen on terrible times and are in desperate want of money. What crime will you commit, and how would you use me to represent and free you?"

"The best method to employ Godfrey, dear, would be one in which I am certain I would never need your services!"

"Indeed! And how do you propose to ensure that?"

"I do everything through third parties of third parties."

"Explain yourself."

"Those under me go somewhere they are not known by a single soul, and there, they find those like me - desperately in want of money, but these people may soon starve without it. Not too lower class. Just those that would believe they were the true masters, but who I could teach to fear repercussion for disloyalty."

"I see! And it is these unfortunate souls you get to rob the bank for you?"

"Rob a bank?! How old-fashioned and rash you are, my love. Robbing a bank, why, I think, sadly, that would be easy. Almost child's play. There is the gold in the vault, all you have to decide is how you are to get at it. The rest is my 'workforce'. Instead, I would want investment. Something that will pay dividends long term. I will start corporations that invite confidence, and then I will tell of ships lost at sea - perhaps not literally but there are so many versions of lost ships. There are always those who can infiltrate an established company and balance the books in a way that makes so many pennies overlooked. I will employ the most dazzling of beauties to cry in the face of men they have just met, and beg for just a little contribution to a great tragedy that has befallen them and left them near destitute. A share of such would come to me in payment for fine clothes, good lodgings and an ever-changing name. If you plan such things correctly, there should be no end to the flowing money stream... This is all if I were desperate and disposed to do such things of course."

"But you have not answered the question. If you truly were, what would you do? What would your first great crime be?"

I went away and scribbled notes on a page, recalling things I had seen, and accosted him not two hours later. "I have figured out how I would commit my very first crime. Just one to get me started and, for your tastes - it is a bank! An English bank that a friend of mine frequented, and I became familiar with it. I have decided how I would rob it, who I would get to do the work for me, how they would operate and how they could best place themselves to do such things. They would burn my letters after my instructions. If I was betrayed, why, I am here and they are there, and they cannot touch me. If they do not give me my share for my part, then I threaten them with my other acquaintances, who would doubtless wish for some of the fortune as payment for such services."

My husband chuckled. "You make me glad you are my wife and not a criminal mastermind. Tell me, do you see any drawback or potential flaw in your plan?"

I thought for some moments. "Only one. That I should be named at all. I should introduce myself to my old acquaintance as if I am an entirely new person. I would operate from behind a new name and new personage that only I myself knew was nothing but a veneer. Then, my dear husband, you would never have to defend me in court, for no one would ever call me to account for the crimes of a created being."

He clapped his hands and kissed me once again as if he were proud. We talked and pretended, in a theatrical way, many times, as if I were the greatest villain in Christendom, and he, as my prosecutor, poked holes in my theories, in my defences and alibi and then, as my solicitor, was always coming up with new ways to get me off the hook, even having me convinced I could never have committed the crime.

I don't think anything stirred for him or even made him uncomfortable at the time. It was just talk, a sweet little game between new husband and wife who loved each other very much. He would sometimes catch me unable to sleep at night and when he rolled over and kissed me in our marital bed, I let him sleep and never said that I was awake thinking my way through a problem for him. One that he would never be able to catch me for.

How to commit a crime, and get away with it. Better yet, how to commit crime after crime, week after week, and never even be remotely attached to the thought of it...

But you see, what I never thought at the time, was that God might have a very precise set of scales and that he was listening too closely, knowing me too eager in the game between my husband and I.

Godfrey was er... hired to represent a young man from one of the 'better families'. Old money, family name to raise eyebrows, you know the kind. He was accused of very violent behaviour behind closed doors. I remember Godfrey saying: 'I've met the man, it can't be true.' But the more he pried, as he could not help doing, the more he realised that this young man wore a mask, better than anything Mr. Holmes or myself could attain. A mask of words and good family and vacuous charm. When he dug deeper, Godfrey changed. Wouldn't tell me anything, just that he wanted the case over, and was looking for a way out. He was afraid of something and was trying to hide it from me.

Then he died. There was a scuffle outside one of the law courts and he got involved, trying to bring it to a calm and he ended up stabbed. They told me he would've died very quickly.

Someone else was appointed to the young man's case and I arranged my husband's funeral. We'd had just over a year together. A year. That was when I got a telegram. 'Meet me tomorrow night stop For Godfrey stop'. One or two exchanges back and forth and the next night, I walk into a hotel room and who is standing there, if not Mr. Sherlock Holmes.

It was a surprise, but it was nice change to see him as he'd been described. He has that singular British brand of handsomeness. I wasn't thinking it at the time, not in words, just, maybe acknowledging it. I pretended I hadn't read his friend's work. I didn't want to embarrass him by quoting him. That I knew he thought I had a face a man might die for. You know I've had all kinds of men in my life, but that's the compliment I treasure the most.

He believed my husband's death was a deliberate act. 'You mean, he was murdered'. I had suspected it from the beginning, but it was the first time I spoke it. The young man Godfrey had been representing had been of 'great importance' in a case Sherlock had been involved in, a year or so previously; the young man happened to be in London. But of course, to avoid a scandal and any political fallout - his father is what you'd call Very Important - the family returned to America and there was little Sherlock could do. But now, if I were to only give him permission, he'd get me my justice. I told him that I didn't even know what was to become of me next, I didn't know if I could stay in my house, if I would have to leave, how much money I now had, who would take me in if it came to it and who would reject me...

And he said... He said: "No one in his senses would ever be able to reject you." And he asked again if he could take the case. Money was not important, as much as ensuring that justice was done. Others needed justice still. "So I'm part of some duty of yours now," I said. "How strangely the world turns." "And yet," he responded, "if it had been anyone else, I would not have crossed an ocean before receiving permission." He got his permission.

I don't know what he did, but he did it all fast. A few days, I think it took, for him to assemble all the evidence that he needed and present it to the right people. I was scared for him. I told him so. "These are dangerous people, Sherlock". "Yes, they are. And yet they are afraid of me."

It was true. They tried a number of things but Sherlock was like a dog with a bone. That - creature, that 'man' - had done whatever he wanted to whoever he wanted for years. They hushed it up, kept it out of the public gaze for years, and he thought Daddy's dollar could always save him. They got rid of Godfrey because of how bad it would look, such a prominent lawyer, newly emigrated, turning down his case. Godfrey's own conscience killed him, it turns out. But that disturbed, arrogant, devil of a man will never know freedom again. And I prefer it that way. That he lives a life abhorrent to him, where he can't hurt people. Same day that I heard the verdict in court? That was the first day in so long that I danced. I danced even though there were tears in my eyes and I danced with Sherlock Holmes. I know! I could barely believe it in the moment, I can barely believe it now. Moreover, we had a glass of wine, though I'm sure I had more than he, and I tried to get him to stay, just for a while longer. 'There's so much that this country could do with your mind and your talents'. "That's very true," he said in his modest way, "but this is not my country. Your country is the one that you love most, and I was very blessed to be born into that which I do."

Next morning, I went to say Goodbye, but he was already gone. So like him. Infuriating man.

He wrote to me on his return. He's not a man of many words on paper. I replied, and I don't know how but we started writing all the time. Sometimes I wouldn't hear from him for weeks - a gripping case, no doubt. Sometimes the ink had barely dried on the letter I'd sent to him, than I got his response. Is it not the strangest thing in the world that you can find a kindred spirit in the last place you thought you'd find them?

And one day, I don't know, I just wrote him a postcard, it simply said:

SH,
Do you ever wish you'd stayed?
IN

I didn't expect anything in return. I just wanted it out there, I just wanted it said. Eventually, I got a reply.

I,
Every day, but I never could've.
S

Oh for god's sake. Why did I even come? Why am I even telling you any of this? You know you have one of those faces. One that makes people just talk to you, I bet. I didn't mean to unburden myself on you. Do you want to know what I think? I think you're doing what I'm doing. You're sitting there hoping that the other person is going to give up and leave first, but you know what, my dear, I've worked as an actress. Waiting is something I have down to a fine art.

Except when it comes to Sherlock Holmes.

She laughs.

I just couldn't resist. His letters sometimes talked about how bored he was, and how his life, like mine, hadn't exactly been what he had hoped it would be. I had received the full sum of my husband's inheritance, much to my still-living in-laws annoyance, for I've no doubt they blamed me for Godfrey's passing even more than I did myself.

And I don't know why... One day, I was just sitting at my desk, reading back over Sherlock's last letter and this idea just popped into my head, and it wouldn't go away. Why not, I thought? Why shouldn't I? Won't it give him a little stimulation? So I wrote back, and asked about someone. I'd never met him, this person, but I'd heard of him. If you'd been in the right circles, we'd all heard something of him, even if we weren't aware he was the one behind the scenes. Several of my friends back in London had had some intercourse with him, and he sounded an awful, frightening character. Had the gentleman in question ever made himself to known to him? Of course, he wanted to know more: who? When? What? How much? That kind of thing.

I gave the name. Strangely, for the feeling of darkness and frightening intelligence it invoked, I had thought it a beautiful name. I didn't say so much in the letter, but I pled that a name, aside from all I had told him, was all I knew. That was all anyone seemed to know. I'd never seen him. He seemed more ghost than real person, acting through a series of men he used like puppets to do his bidding. What their goal was seemed simple in the moment, but surely they were all part of some great game their invisible master was playing. These pawns, these men's names? Well, I had very little idea about that. Besides, here was I, on the other side of the globe: what was it to do with me? I knew so little! I had only asked in passing.

I went too far. I always go too far.

No sooner had I given this second letter to my girl than I knew my hook had a catch. I write at once to an old acquaintance of mine 'I have something I want you to do. It's intricate but clever, and if you do exactly as I say, the two of us could be very rich indeed. Here's my idea. Follow it to the letter.'

I daresay he didn't understand, but then you should never forget if you've ever wronged a woman in any way - we have very long memories - or otherwise, I'll set my English greyhound on you. He deserved his prison sentence. Sherlock got him. I gave him to him. And god, that was a thrill.

But once the game was started, I couldn't stop. The ideas that I had had, for years now, problems I had given myself while lying awake in Godfrey's bed - if I were to commit the perfect crime, how might it be done - they came bubbling up like a spring. I ran out of paper making notes for schemes. Nothing serious, I told myself. Yet I was consumed. I played this part that Sherlock needed me to play better than any I ever did on the stage...

Do you know what it's like to have stepped onto a stage in front of hundreds of people? To have sang your heart out, and meant every word, in front of so many souls. To stand with your arms raised for gracious applause and out across an auditorium and you realise they are not just clapping; they are standing. They honour you and the way for a brief space of time you have made them feel. Kings and Queens themselves have shouted 'bravo!' from their box and you believe in the power of the moment that such a feeling could never end and then... Then years have passed. The auditorium is quiet and empty. No applause, no calls for encore. You have grown old and even those who professed to love and worship you forever one night, years ago... they could pass you in the street and never know who you are.

But then... you have the attention of one man. One important, fiercely intelligent man. He alone sits in the auditorium. He alone can see and hear you now. Not just your song, but your mind. For the first time, you realise you don't wear a mask, no, you are seen! It is you he applauds and celebrates and would raise his glass to.

And if he could see your face he would know your greatness, in a way no one before, kings nor your zealots could know...

One. One person who fascinates you, but they're just out of reach. Yet both of you are feeding off each other, like you're on narcotics. I organised and wrote letters, day after day, in the middle of the night, found scoundrel after referred scoundrel who would take the fall. Eventually, I was so taken with my new work, there was nothing else for it. I rented the house and I moved back across the ocean. From here, I could make things even more difficult, even more complex. Sherlock had to work; I made sure of it.

And yet every time I wrote him, as myself, I kept right on asking, as if I had only just remembered the minute before I finished the letter. Oh and Sherlock, any more news on that Moriarty character?

I went too far. Far, far too far. But finally, I saw it all. I felt it. My potential and all that had been denied me, all my life, trapped in this body where I was overlooked. Nothing but a plaything for the rich when I was young. Now they were my playthings. Now I was the puppetmaster - anyone with a secret, anyone with something to lose or desperate enough to make a blunder, I could make them do what I wanted.

And by the time I realised... by the time I remembered that the whole reason any of this had started, was simply to give Sherlock something of real worth to do - something worthy of his mind, just as I had been searching for years for something and never even known it - by the time I understood that even he was at my mercy, that I could very well ruin his career, maybe even destroy the man himself if he realised that I'd trounced him not just the once but many times. That I too could play with people like they were my puppets. It was all far too late. I'd gone too far, too far to turn back.

I had a letter forwarded to me. He was worried. He didn't need to say so much, but he stated in a hand that was almost a shaking version of his own that he hadn't heard from me in a long while, thought I'd been... gotten to. Oh god, I'd have given anything to take it all back, to undo it, just in that moment.

I sat with the letter in my lap in my back garden, the note struck, wondering what to do, when my girl comes out and you could have knocked me down with a feather: "Mr. Sherlock Holmes to see you, Ma'am."

She assumes the role of Sherlock seamlessly, portraying the conversation between the two.

By the time my surprise had allowed me to rise from the chaise, he was already standing there, and his face, that infuriating British face of his, told me everything I could question. "This all has to stop. It has gone far enough, and it must end, immediately."

"How long have you known?" I asked.

"Oh, I suspected from the beginning," he said. "I found it highly unlikely that even in your circles, you'd heard of a, what was the phrase you used? A 'Napoleon' of crime?"

"I was rather proud of that turn of phrase."

"Hmm. It has a certain ring to it. But I can't overlook things any more. Even with you not being the direct perpetrator of any of this, your goading has put you in serious danger."

"You can't make an honest man a criminal, no matter what. None of these men were honest."

"And as Moriarty, neither are you. Is this not all a little... beneath you?"

You know, the king of Bohemia couldn't have made me feel so small and ridiculous as he did then. "What do you intend to do?" I asked. "I'm certain there's something you could make stick, for all of how careful I've been."

"If you had been careful, I would not be here." Like a schoolmaster and a wayward student. "But actually, there might be a way in which we could help one another, and the only thing you have to do is to say nothing."

And he talked. Told me about his 'plan' for 'Moriarty. Told me how London was too much, and Watson's stories could sometimes be too much and other people and their idiocy and their duplicity and their just damned irrational, repetitive humanity were too much. He wanted to get away.

"Are you asking me to keep Moriarty alive so you can 'get away'?"

"No, not in the slightest. I'm telling you to. Here, we help each other out of an extraordinarily awkward situation. You from prison, myself from mediocrity. What is your response?"

"Sherlock, I'm under no illusion that you're giving me a choice."

"Then, Irena, we understand one another."

God damn, I hate that man.

I was really sort of hoping he hadn't actually gone. He's feeding something to that dogsbody of his to make the whole thing more plausible, he's hired actors and everything! No, actually, I'm really very cross with him. Very cross. Because even with all this, I've no idea where he is! You think he'd tell me, after the stunt I've been pulling for over a year? After I crossed a continent for a prank and got people arrested by doing what I asked? I don't know where he is. He could be out of London. He might be on a train or a ship out of the country. To get his own back, he could be taking himself off to America. Or, maybe just to humiliate me all the more, *(reaching a crescendo)* I wouldn't put it past Sherlock Holmes to be hiding in this very room right at this very minute, and neither you nor I would have a single clue about it! Goddamn, I hate that man!

And - and you know why?! You know why? Why, because... because he... because he makes everyone else seem so pallid and colourless and trivial. Why am I here? I'll tell you why I'm really here. I'm here because I sort of hoped that he hadn't really gone. And if he hadn't, then we could talk, like this. I could speak now. I could tell him, it hasn't been all that I've had in my life, recently. Just the most entertaining. But you should have seen us dance together.

So I don't think he's coming back tonight. Or for a long time, so I hope it wasn't an urgent business you had... He'll come back at some point, when he's bored, probably, but only when he's good and ready...

A thought has come to her. She comes to the edge of the stage and peers out as if looking at someone...

Forgive me. For a split second, I had the most outrageous thought.

What did you say your name was?... Well, it was as nice as it was frustrating to make your acquaintance, I'm sure. Sure you want to wait?   I can walk you out.... Suit yourself. I'm trusting your discretion and the fact that if you told anyone, they'd never believe you anyway. Besides, people who cross me aren't always as lucky as Sherlock. And, er, just in case... If you do see him, tell him... Tell him I hope he has a backlog of cases... because I still didn't get to use my best ideas.

Goodnight, whoever you are. In the nicest possible way, let's hope we never see each other again...

With an ethereal swish, she sweeps from the stage with poise, as the lights very slowly dim.

A few moments after she departs, the armchair moves ever so slightly, as if someone has been hiding behind it...

Curtain.

ACKNOWLEDGEMENTS

Thanks - of a sort - as I am ever obliged to dispense to my side-kick and pain-in-my-side-for-a-variety-of-reasons, Andrew Slade, who said he'd help me with this book and then left me to do everything but the book formatting and audio editing on my own. I finished this whole thing of turning the play into a book predominantly riding a wave of spite and See-If-I-Don't, so there's that. Yet at least you've kept me going through the darkest hours, like a Watson. A Boswell. A Dawson from Basil The Great Mouse Detective.

My husband Artie. My knight in over-the-top, anime armour. You put up with so much and so rarely complain, considering all that you take on and do. You have made life worth living again despite my infirmities, my conditions and my borderline insanity, some of which is definitely self-induced. Thank you for seeing the good in me even when I was convinced there was none.

Thank you and blessings to Bik, Jan, and everyone who belonged to the Southampton Art House, through whom Baker Street Ladies joined its sister plays in having its debut there. I doubt I would have half so much confidence in my own one-woman and self-penned shows were it not for all your kindness, encouragement, and faith in saying "Come! Do a thing!" each time I had a new project idea.

ABOUT THE AUTHOR/ PLAYWRIGHT

Alexandra (Lexi) Wolfe is originally a Sheffield native but who grew up between the Steel City and Multan in Pakistan. She graduated from Liverpool with a degree in Creative and Performing Arts and has a Masters from the Liverpool Institute of Performing Arts in Acting. She has written a number of other books, her first being a vampire one in 2013 (*Better Off Dead: The Story of Rosa The Fledgling Vampire*), a more recent one being a collection of her own ghost stories (*It's Haunted, They Said*), and others mostly revolving around her stage plays and poetry. She lives with her husband Artie in Folkestone, and a retired-racer greyhound called Mark, who she co-parents with her friend Andrew.